Venture
to the Smokies 🐾

A Teddy Bear Explores
Great Smoky Mountains National Park

As told to Sloan Heermance

Dedicated to Children

May the wonders
and beauty of nature
fill their lives.

Published by Venture's Adventures, LLC
2406 Lawrence Street
Eugene, OR 97405-2660
www.venturesadventures.com

ISBN: 978-0-9796467-0-6
Library of Congress Control Number:
2007929998

Printed in Hong Kong

Acknowledgements

My heartfelt thanks to:

Larry Deckman: for a shared lifetime of love, growth, creativity, editing, and for always supporting the efforts of Venture.

Sharon Franklin: for editing and nurturing the voice of our favorite bear.

Skye Blaine: for the playful, initial layout design that helped me see what a book could be.

Beverly Soasey: for the final, creative layout in which Venture grew into being.

Dana Hansler: for first introducing me to Venture, instilling a love of travel in him, and wrapping him in creative clothing.

Diane Wooldridge: for creating a "chip off the old block" while designing Little V.

Steve Kemp: for giving the book direction and guidance along the way.

Karen Ballentine: for suggestions and offering the names of excellent reviewers.

Judy Dulin, Jennifer Webster, and Carey Jones: for reviewing the book, catching flaws, making improvements, and participating in the creative process.

Katie Settlage: for taking Venture to see a real bear den and verifying bear information.

Many Others: for helping and encouraging me along the way.

Photo Credits: Bill Lea: iv (otter, bear), v (elk), 2, 3 (river), 3 (bear), 12 (bear), 16 (turkey), 17 (rabbit), 19 (bear), 56, 57 (bears), 58 (bear), 63 (Grotto Falls), 65, 66 (elk), 70, 71 (pileated woodpecker), 73, 76, 78 (river otter), 83 (monarch butterfly), 94 (tree), 102 (groundhog), 112 & back cover (mountains)

National Park Service: 12 (squirrel), 13 (fawn), 14 (barred owl), 24, 27 (squirrel), 25, 26 (turtle), 37 (laurel), 38 (Laurel Falls) 40, 42 (green frog), 64 (mink), 84, 85 (salamander), 99 (winter scene)

Bill Beatty: 49, 50 (firefly)

Great Smoky Mountains National Park

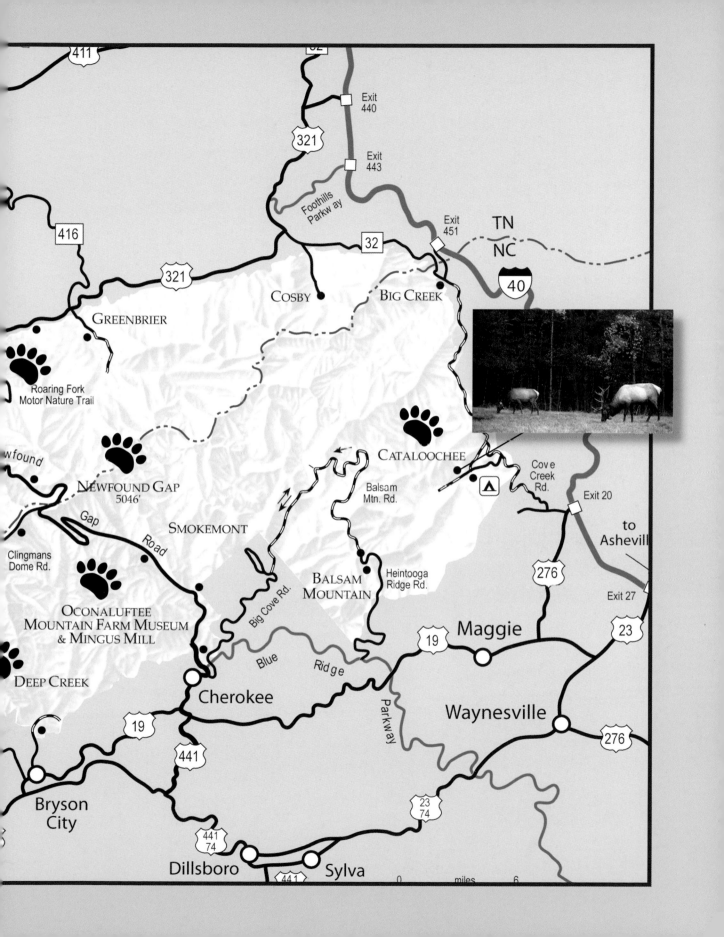

411

Exit 440

321

Exit 443

Foothills Parkway

416

32

Exit 451

TN
NC

321

I-40

COSBY   BIG CREEK

GREENBRIER

Roaring Fork
Motor Nature Trail

CATALOOCHEE

Cove
Creek
Rd.

Balsam
Mtn. Rd.

Exit 20

Newfound

NEWFOUND GAP
5046'

SMOKEMONT

Heintooga
Ridge Rd.

to
Asheville

276

Gap

Road

BALSAM
MOUNTAIN

Exit 27

Clingmans
Dome Rd.

OCONALUFTEE
MOUNTAIN FARM MUSEUM
& MINGUS MILL

Big Cove Rd.

23

Maggie

19

DEEP CREEK

Blue   Ridge

Waynesville

Cherokee

Parkway

276

19

441

23
74

Bryson
City

441
74

0   miles   6

Dillsboro   Sylva

441

Great Smoky Mountains National Park
United States

Kentucky

Virginia

Great Smoky Mountains
National Park

Tennessee

North Carolina

Georgia

South
Carolina

Table of Contents

Chapter 1
Pleased to Meet You

Allow me to introduce myself.

My name is Venture and I'm a traveling teddy bear. As you can tell by my name (short for adventure), I'm always ready to explore.

As bears go, I'm not very big. On my tiptoes I stand just ten inches tall. What is big, though, is my curiosity. I love to see the wonders of nature. I love to learn new and exciting things.

My favorite place to explore is Great Smoky Mountains National Park. It is in two states, Tennessee and North Carolina. A smoky haze covers the park's beautiful mountains. This smoky haze gives the mountains their name.

1

In the Great Smokies, rushing waterfalls, rivers, and streams flow through forests filled with plants and animals. Some life forms live only in this park and nowhere else on earth!

Because it is a national park, people protect and care for the park's natural world.

The park also preserves human history. The Cherokee

Indians and non-Indian families once lived on the land. Here they farmed, hunted, and lived closely with nature. In the park you can sit on an old front porch and imagine how people lived on this land more than one hundred years ago.

One reason I love the park is that it is home to more than 1,000 black bears. I think of bears as my long lost cousins, so I am always on the lookout for them.

My latest adventure was the best ever. Here is a list of what I took. I turned out to be a good packer. Everything came in handy.

- ☑ Backpack
- ☑ Journal
- ☑ Binoculars
- ☑ Flashlight
- ☑ Rain gear
- ☑ National parks' passport
- ☑ First-aid kit
- ☑ Tent
- ☑ Sunscreen
- ☑ Snacks

- ☑ Camera
- ☑ Pencils
- ☑ Hand lens
- ☑ Water bottle
- ☑ Hat
- ☑ Whistle
- ☑ Insect repellent
- ☑ Sleeping bag
- ☑ Maps
- ☑ Hot chocolate

Of course I also brought my sense of wonder. You always need that when you "venture" to Great Smoky Mountains National Park!

Fun Facts About Great Smoky Mountains National Park

- It is the most visited national park in the U.S.
- The park has ½ million acres of land.
- More than 100,000 different life forms live in the park and new kinds are discovered each year.
- You can see more than 130 different kinds of trees.
- Many children collected pennies and nickels to help pay for this park.

Activity Page

Word Scramble
Packing

Unscramble some of the words from
my packing list on page 4.

1. PAMS   __ __ __ __

2. SEPNLCI   __ __ __ __ __ __ __

3. OTH LAETOCOHC   __ __ __ __ __ __ __ __ __ __ __ __

4. LNRJUOA   __ __ __ __ __ __ __

5. CBKAKACP   __ __ __ __ __ __ __ __

6. RUISAOLBCN   __ __ __ __ __ __ __ __ __

7. NETT   __ __ __ __

8. ITALFLHHSG   __ __ __ __ __ __ __ __ __ __

9. AHT   __ __ __

10. RCAEAM   __ __ __ __ __ __

Activity Page

Color the States

1. Can you find Tennessee and North Carolina on the map? Color them in and label them.
2. What state do you live in? Color it and label it.
3. Mark Great Smoky Mountains National Park with an **X**.

Spring

Chapter 2

Oh, the Places I'll See

I started my big adventure at the Sugarlands Visitor Center. It's a great place to learn about the Smokies. First I watched a movie about the national park. Then I got a Junior Ranger activity book to become a Junior Ranger. Like park rangers, Junior Rangers help protect the Smokies so they stay beautiful for generations to come.

After that, a park ranger stamped my passport to the national parks, and I asked her for ideas of fun things to do. Her suggestions made my toes wiggle with excitement. Of course, I added a few ideas of my own.

❒ Take a hayride.

❒ Go on a hike.

❒ Go horseback riding.

❒ Drink hot chocolate *(my idea)*.

❒ Take a night hike.

❒ Go bike riding.

❒ Camp out.

❒ Take pictures.

❒ Go bird watching.

❒ Fish for trout.

❒ Gaze at the stars.

❒ Watch fireflies.

❒ Search for bears.

There were so many exciting things to do. The ranger showed me a map of places to visit. She asked me many questions.

"Do you want to see mountain views?"
Yes.
"Do you want to visit waterfalls?"
Yes.
"Do you want to walk in meadows?"
Yes.
"Do you want to see old trees, wildflowers, and salamanders?"
Yes! Yes! Yes!
I wanted it all!

But most of all I wanted to see bears, so I asked the ranger where the bears might be. She smiled and said, "They are everywhere and could be anywhere there's food. Sometimes you see them. Sometimes you don't." Then she winked and added, "But Cades Cove is a good place to start."

I went home to my cabin and listened to the nighttime songs of toads, frogs, and katydids. I also marked the places I wanted to visit on my park map with small bear-paw stickers.

Cades Cove was first on my list. When I went to bed, I couldn't get Cades Cove out of my mind. I tossed and turned, wondering, *Would I see any bears?*

Activity Page

Word Search
Places to See and Things to Do

```
Y B O R A S P P M Q A C L C Q G F X K F
D G V O X G X M H I K E G N V R I O H E
I X I O A S U G A R L A N D S T S T R Q
R M O L D O S N O U U V F P N B H S K D
X C D M N V J C R N I E A S Q W Y G J R
Q A T Y H L A U R E L F A L L S Y Z P E
X M X U T C A D E S C O V E Y Z H O B X
E P P F U B Z M H V Y F W F X H W N A K
K E B U Y Y Q T Z D M I J K V L A D C X
R O A R I N G F O R K A M C D G M Q T N
G Y N E W F O U N D G A P E K I W W W R
T V L I U L A B D U N W I W Y M U J U T
M H O R S E B A C K R I D E V Y Y P R U
A L O T E C A X D K U V I E S D Q G C E
C Z A C R W L F K C F M Y X T W H R D L
V S W D P L R W D E E P C R E E K F E E
L D N P H R O I A B R A M S F A L L S F
K A G J Y I J M M K F N C E R C O N B O
W J W I L Q H M S X S N H E Z K S P H A
K V Y L D S T A R G A Z E N C M H A X G
```

Cades Cove	hike	camp	Laurel Falls
Sugarlands	horseback ride	fish	Newfound Gap
stargaze	Roaring Fork	Deep Creek	Abrams Falls

Activity Page

Maze
The Places I'll Go

Help Venture find a path
through the maze to see a bear.

**Venture
Starts**

End

**Venture
sees a
bear!**

Spring

Chapter 3

Cades Cove

I awoke to a foggy spring morning. Dewdrops hung on the branches of the dogwood trees. Even in my fluffy fur coat, I shivered in the chilly air.

I stuffed my backpack with an extra sweater and set off for my day trip to Cades Cove.

The cove is a lovely, lush valley on the western side of the park. Just as the fog began to clear, I saw a spotted fawn.

A family of coyotes sped off across the meadow and quickly disappeared into the woods. I had come to the right place for wildlife.

I wandered along a trail and found a place to sit. I poured myself some hot chocolate and settled in. After a while I noticed an interesting shape on the ground in the distance. I focused my binoculars and found myself staring into the dark brown eyes of a barred owl. What a surprise! It swiveled its head almost all the way around and called out something that sounded like *Who cooks for you? Who cooks for you?*

The owl made me think about food, and that led me to Cable Mill just down the road. Cable Mill is a wonderful place to learn about how people lived in the past. Built in the 1860s, the mill still grinds corn into flour using waterpower and a giant grinding stone.

As I watched the water wheel turn, images of warm cornbread with melted butter for dinner rushed into my mind. My empty tummy rumbled, but cornbread would have to wait.

Now it was time for a hayride! I headed to the stables a few miles away. I climbed up into the truck (not an easy thing for a little bear to do) and nestled into the pile of hay for my tour around the cove.

We passed a flock of wild turkeys. Red wattles hung on the throats of the males and I could hear them gobbling when the truck stopped for a moment. I laughed to myself when I thought about funny turkey words like *wattle* and *gobble*. Even the word *turkey* tickled me. I wondered where all those words came from.

As we continued to bounce down the road, I noticed a cottontail rabbit in the field. It stood on its hind legs and seemed to be watching for danger. A hawk soared high above in the sky and I knew the rabbit might be in trouble. Maybe it saw the hawk too, because it turned and ran away, showing the white side of its tail.

The hayride was lots of fun, but I still hadn't seen any bears. Once the ride ended, I decided to search for them in the woods. This turned out to be a great idea.

As I walked, I noticed what looked like small ears of corn on the ground. My wildflower book said that it was squawroot and that bears like to eat it. Were any bears around?

I remembered that in the spring, black bears spend a lot of time in trees eating buds and insects. With this in mind, I decided to lie down on the ground, get comfortable, and point my binoculars straight up. I scanned the trees carefully. Up the trunk, over the branches, I focused my binoculars and looked around.

A dark spot caught my eye. High up in the branches I saw a little black bear cub! It had big ears, a long snout, and curious eyes. I don't think it knew what to make of a teddy bear like me. It turned its head and sniffed the air. It seemed to wonder, are you a bear?

I watched the cub stretch out its paws. I could see the sharp claws it uses to climb and dig. I wondered if the cub's den (the place it was born) was nearby. Then I heard the grunting noise of its mother calling. The cub quickly disappeared into the tree. It was definitely the bear's home.

It was time for me to return to my den too. I went home, spread melted butter on warm cornbread, and felt grateful for my wonder-filled day in Cades Cove. What a great place!

Fun Facts About Bear Cubs

- Bears come out of their dens in the spring.
- In years when there is plenty of food in the summer and fall, mother bears are likely to have many cubs. They might have two, three, or even four.
- Cubs stay with their mothers for a year and a half. During that time they learn how to find food and stay safe.
- A bear cub in trouble can sound like a human baby crying.

Activity Page

Venture's Favorite Cornbread

Make Venture's favorite cornbread recipe with an adult.

Ingredients:

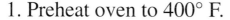

1 cup sifted all-purpose flour

1/4 cup sugar

4 teaspoons baking powder

3/4 teaspoons salt

1 cup yellow cornmeal

2 eggs

1 cup milk

1/4 cup shortening

1. Preheat oven to 400° F.
2. Oil an 8-inch square baking dish.
3. Mix all liquid ingredients together.
4. Mix all dry ingredients together.
5. Add dry ingredients to liquid ingredients.
6. Stir until blended.
7. Pour into baking dish.
8. Bake in preheated oven for 25-30 minutes, or until done.
9. Spread with butter and honey. Yummm!

Activity Page

Put Them in Order

Can you put the recipe steps in the right order without looking? What comes first? Place the number 1 by the first thing to do and continue to 9. Now, check your answers with the recipe on page 20. Don't peek!

__ Spread with butter and honey.
__ Stir until blended.
__ Pour into baking dish.
__ Preheat oven to 400° F.
__ Mix all dry ingredients together.
__ Oil an 8-inch square baking dish.
__ Bake in preheated oven for 25-30 minutes, or until done.
__ Mix all liquid ingredients together.
__ Add dry ingredients to liquid ingredients.

Activity Page

Crossword
Cades Cove

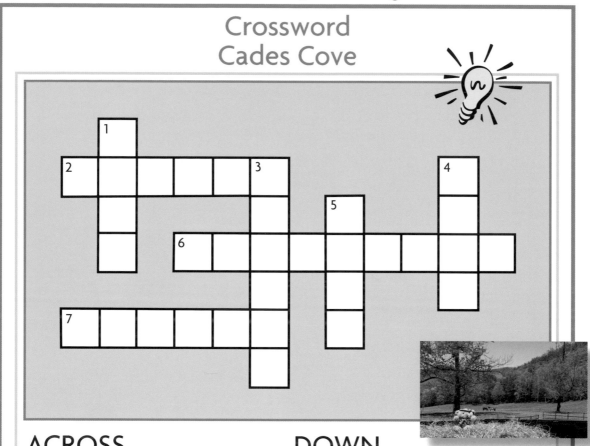

ACROSS

2. hops on long hind legs

6. its call sounds like
   "who cooks for you"

7. a wild member of the
   dog family

DOWN

1. a bird of prey

3. makes a gobbling sound

4. a deer less than one year old

5. often has a den in a tree

Spring

Chapter 4

Small Wonders on a Quiet Walkway

One night, sharp flashes of silver light woke me out of a sound sleep. Lightning crackled in the sky. Thunder rumbled and seemed to shake the hills. I drifted back to sleep and woke to heavy rain in the morning.

While I waited for the weather to clear, I decided to work in my Junior Ranger book. One activity said to look at nature with a hand lens, so when it stopped raining, I set out to discover the wonderful world of small things.

A Quiet Walkway would be perfect. The park has many trails marked "Quiet Walkway" that are great for exploring. On these trails visitors can stroll slowly and find places to be alone in nature. I chose one in the cool forest with lots of flowers all around.

A red squirrel with its colorful, bushy tail chattered above me. It seemed to warn all the woodland creatures that I was entering their world. Maybe it wanted to scare me away from its maple syrup tree. Do you know that red squirrels chew into trees to let the sweet sap ooze out?

I found a spot by a small stream and examined flowers with my hand lens. As I stared into the center of one, it reminded me of a group of dancers. Another looked like the rays of a star.

Each flower was so beautiful that I took out a pencil and started to draw them in my journal.

I was lost in my art when I heard something rustle on the forest floor. I turned my head toward the sound and saw a colorful box turtle crawl out of the dirt and leaves. Its shell, with bright orange markings, moved slowly toward me.
I had company! Maybe it wanted to see an artist at work, or maybe it came out because it was starting to rain. Box turtles like wet weather.

Small, wet drops began to dot my page, so I put away my tools and started for home. Later that night I finished the last page of my Junior Ranger book and stepped outside for fresh air. Tiny golden lights twinkled in the dark. I happily added fireflies (also called lightning bugs) to the small wonders of my day.

Fun Facts About Box Turtles

- Box turtles grow to be six inches long.
- They eat berries, mushrooms, earthworms, slugs, snails, and insects like grasshoppers and crickets.
- They can live to be thirty or forty years old. Some live to be one hundred.
- The females usually dig their nests on stormy evenings.

Activity Page

Through a Hand Lens

Look at some things in nature with a hand lens.
Draw what you see. What does it remind you of?

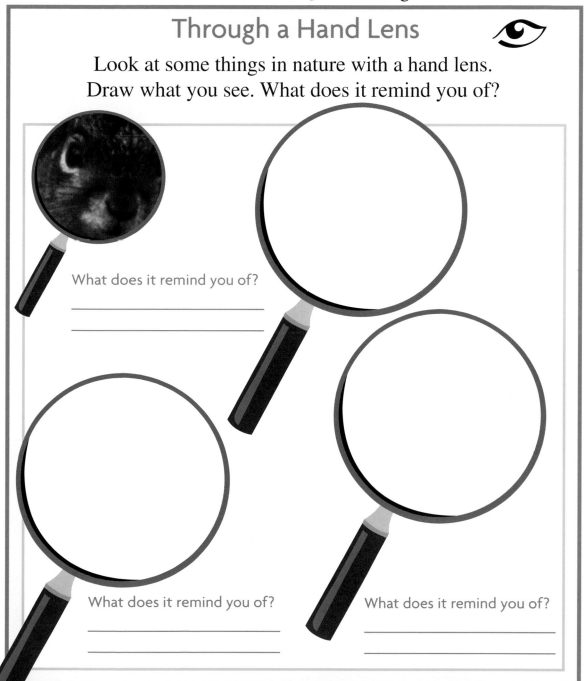

What does it remind you of?

_____

_____

What does it remind you of?

_____

_____

What does it remind you of?

_____

_____

Activity Page

Use Your Senses

Take a quiet hike with a grown up. Use your senses.

What do you see?

_____

_____

_____

_____

What do you hear?

_____

_____

_____

_____

What do you smell?

_____

_____

_____

_____

What do you feel?

_____

_____

_____

_____

Spring

Chapter 5

Back in Time

I woke up one spring morning and decided it was time to visit the old cabins and land of the farm families that lived in the park many years ago. After breakfast I tidied up and set out for the Mountain Farm Museum in Oconaluftee, North Carolina.

The Mountain Farm Museum isn't an ordinary indoor museum. It's a whole farm with historic buildings. When you wander there, you feel like you have traveled back in time.

I sat on the old porch of the farmhouse and imagined myself living there in the 1800s. I walked around and looked at the woodshed, the meat house, the beehives, and chicken house.

I thought of all the hard work people had to do on a farm back then—and all without electricity!

Here is what a **To Do List** from those days might have looked like.

✓ Plow soil.
✓ Grow crops.
✓ Store vegetables.

✓ Cut down trees.
✓ Saw lumber.
✓ Build cabin.

✓ Chop wood.
✓ Stack wood.
✓ Keep fire going.

✓ Butcher hog.
✓ Smoke meat.
✓ Salt pork.

✓ Check beehives.
✓ Feed chickens.
✓ Collect eggs.

I also visited the apple house, the corncrib, the blacksmith shop, and the barn. The list of chores went on.

✓ Gather apples.
✓ Dry apples.
✓ Make cider.

✓ Shuck corn.
✓ Grind corn.
✓ Bake bread.

✓ Shoe horses.
✓ Make tools.
✓ Repair tools.

✓ Feed animals.
✓ Milk cows.
✓ Make butter.

✓ Haul water.
✓ Heat water.
✓ Wash clothes.

Busy.
Busy.
Busy.

After all that "work," I needed a hot chocolate break. Refreshed, I headed to Noah Bud Ogle's house near Roaring Fork. He was one of the early settlers in the Smokies. I found his old cabin, barn, and mill by the water. I strolled on his land and imagined what his life with his family had been like.

I felt quite at home at Old Bud's. I sat and sketched and thought about the fun things his family might have done on the farm.

* Breathe fresh air.
* Drink clean water.
* Smell the earth.

* Hear the bees.
* Climb fruit trees.
* Listen to frogs.

* Gaze at stars.
* Watch the moon.
* Nap in the sun.

* Build strong muscles.
* Ride a horse.
* Play in the stream.

* Make a whistle.
* Shoot marbles.
* Play hide and seek.

Fun.
Fun.
Fun.

* Sing songs.
* Play the fiddle.
* Dance the night away.

What a pleasure it was to drift back in time. As the sun set, I said goodbye to the cabin and life in the olden days.

I was one tired teddy bear. I went home to sleep and dream.

Activity Page

Back in Time

Imagine yourself back in time. Where are you living?
What are you doing? Draw a picture and describe your life.

Draw it:

Describe it:

_____

_____

_____

_____

_____

Activity Page

Word Scramble
Work and Play on the Farm

1. YLPA   — — — —

2. IDRE   — — — —

3. DEACN   — — — — —

4. FEDE   — — — —

5. KBAE   — — — —

6. BDLIU   — — — — —

7. IMLK   — — — —

8. NPA   — — —

9. CILBM   — — — — —

10. HOPC   — — — —

11. POWL   — — — —

12. AGZE   — — — —

Spring

Chapter 6
The Big Event of My Day

Heavy rain poured from the sky in the morning. The rain would help fill all the streams, rivers, and waterfalls that keep animals and plants in the Smokies alive. It seemed like the perfect day to travel along Little River Road and pay my respects to the life-giving water. As it turned out, the road would lead me to the Big Event of my day.

Along the way I stopped and hiked to Laurel Falls. As I climbed upward on the path, I peered into lovely mountain laurel flowers that looked like tiny, delicate teacups. I could imagine insects and birds drinking from them.

I heard the rush of falling water in the distance. I followed its musical sound and soon arrived at the falls. Water spilled on the rocks and tumbled over the hillside. I took deep breaths of the moist air and felt great. Laurel Falls is a place not to be missed.

After hiking to the falls, I continued on beautiful Little River Road. The road has many curves and plenty of things to see around each bend.

I noticed water-loving Canada geese and stopped to enjoy them. The mother and father watched over their fearless young ones. The tiny goslings sure needed protection as they walked beside a well-traveled road. Luckily, they had parents to guard them.

I traveled along the road until a place near the water seemed to call to me. I found a spot to sit by the edge of the river and listened to its soothing, lullaby music. Then I heard something like the plunking of a banjo string. It sounded like *glunk, glunk, glunk*.

I crept slowly toward the sound, but every time I moved, it stopped. When I stopped, it started again, but it seemed to come from a totally different direction. What was making that sound, and where was it coming from? Step by step, I continued my search.

Just as I was ready to give up, something leapt out of the bushes. There I stood, face to face with a green frog! *Glunk, glunk, glunk,* it called, as its throat swelled and contracted. I had found the "banjo player."

I could have watched that frog for a long time, but I needed to leave the river for the Big Event of my day. I headed to Cades Cove to meet with a park ranger.

Ranger Mike met me at the Visitor Center with a bright, friendly smile. I proudly took out my finished Junior Ranger book and showed it to him. Ranger Mike's eyes sparkled and his face lit up when he saw that I had completed every page.

I raised my right paw, and took my oath.

**As a Junior Ranger,
I promise to help protect
the plants and animals
of Great Smoky Mountains National Park
and keep the air, water, and land clean.
I will continue to learn more about the park
so that I can help protect it
for all the years to come.**

The smile on Ranger Mike's face widened as he said,
"Congratulations, Venture!" He pinned my new badge on my
vest, making it official. I was now **Venture, Junior Ranger!**

With my badge, I felt like I was wearing an invisible cape with a big V on it. I was Venture, Defender of Great Smoky Mountains National Park. I was Venture, Defender of Clean Water, Frogs, and Goslings.

I was a Junior Ranger. This was indeed the Big Event of my day!

Fun Facts About Green Frogs

- Green frogs have sticky tongues to help capture their food.
- They eat insects, spiders, and snails.
- Larger frogs, turtles, snakes, raccoons, and wading birds eat green frogs.

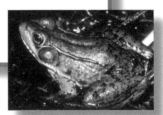

Activity Page

A Big Event

Describe a Big Event in your life.
What made it so special?

Describe:

_____

_____

_____

_____

_____

_____

Draw it:

Activity Page

Word Search
What Green Frogs Eat

```
F N G E I C R A Y F I S H X Y P U H U J
M H I N S E C T S I R M G M O T H S Y K
F E D X X H P I Z W K R N J L H X A W Z
Q G H U K U L O Z D X E A W M G S M L Y
O B E E T L E S A N B Q A S P N C F N H
F N R P V X X F P S R B S E L Q L Q W
T O Y V Z C N L R W X F W P R G P U C R
J H B M D D T I S L U G S I V N U T R G
U I O I P D D E I Y Y H N D U Z A P Y X
B U C W W R C S I R K I C E U N L E B G
B M N C G P B C N Z A X Y R M C F G U J
N X D I R S N A I L S Y K S J V A N T S
S C D K Y C Y M Z S N A K E S J B S V C
B H X H X G B G A U P P F T I D O X X O
F R F D B U T T E R F L I E S J O G Y V
C V C R K O T K M T B W W D R R Y J U L
V E U Q C A T E R P I L L A R S J B A W
L F B C J M R H U X F X H T T O O Z U Q
A C Z H H G A E N D Y F A O A B B T O Y
P H R H Z U T Q C Z D X N D O X N R I X
```

insects	spiders	beetles	ants
slugs	crayfish	flies	caterpillars
butterflies	moths	snakes	snails

Summer

Chapter 7

Night Lights and Summer Songs

The warm August air vibrated with summer songs. Insects rubbed their wings, legs, and other body parts together to create a steady hum and buzz. They called to each other day and night. I decided the best way to listen to nature's music was to camp out.

I left my cabin, traveled to Deep Creek, and set up my tent. I stored my food in a bear-proof can to protect my favorite snacks from black bears. Bears have an excellent sense of smell, and I

didn't want them to raid all my goodies. Bears need to eat what is natural for them, like the yummy berries that are plentiful this time of year.

45

With my camp all tidy, I set off for a nearby stream. I wanted to catch some fish for dinner. Trout would be good, especially "brookies." They are the only trout native to the Smokies.

I put a plastic lure on my line, cast out, and then reeled my line back in. Trout can see shadows and movement, so I stayed as still as I could. I threw out my line again and again, but I didn't get a bite.

All the while a steady *buzz* filled the air. Where was it coming from? I looked up just as a small, black insect flew by and landed on a branch. I peered closely and saw a cicada. He created all this noise by vibrating body parts on his belly. I tried it myself but all I did was ruffle my fur!

I wasn't "catching" anything but the sight of insects, so I decided to try my luck at something else.

After a quick snack I set out for a hike on Juney Whank Trail. Juney Whank means *place where the bear passes* in the Cherokee language. I sure wanted a bear to pass near me.

I hiked up the trail to Juney Whank Falls, looking for berries along the way. Bears eat many kinds of berries, like blackberries, blueberries, and raspberries. I spied huckleberries and picked quite a few. No wonder bears like this trail.

I arrived at the falls and watched the water tumble down the rocks. It seemed like a perfect place for a bear to take a shower.

The sun was setting, but that did not end my summer adventure. I was going on a night hike! I went back to my tent to prepare. I covered my flashlight with red plastic, which is a good thing to do for seeing at night, and filled my pack with snacks. Then I eagerly set off down a trail.

As evening turned into night, my eyes became used to the dark. The night was full of different sounds like *huzzz, chuzzz,* and *chi-di-di-dit, chi-di-di-dit.* Male crickets rubbed their wings and called to females in chirping, trilling songs.

Katydids also called with their wings, sometimes saying *Katy did* and other times calling *Katy didn't.*

As I walked through the woods, tiny spider eyes shined from the bushes. I looked for salamanders, because they usually come out at night. I didn't see any, but a toad hopped across my path and quickly jumped away.

When I came into a clearing, my eyes opened wide with
excitement. Fireflies blinked their bright, golden lights against
the dark sky. The males flitted in the air, "winking" their lights
off and on to the females on the ground.

Do you know that each kind of firefly has its own light patterns
that it uses over and over again? There are even fireflies in the
park that all flash their lights on and off at the same time! That
amazing light show happens at Elkmont in mid-June.

Suddenly, a glowworm on the ground lit up and I stared at the
blue-green light at the tip of its body. A glowworm is a firefly
in its young stage (larva) and it is not really a worm at all.
I focused my flashlight on it and watched it move on tiny
legs. Perhaps it was hunting for dinner. A snail, earthworm,
or slug would make a tasty meal.

Exploring the night was fun. I stretched out on the ground and stared into the star-filled sky. The planets Jupiter and Venus shone brightly above me.

Then I found my favorite constellations. Can you guess what they are? They're the Little Bear and Great Bear, of course. The Little Bear is also called the Little Dipper, and the Great Bear's brightest stars are called the Big Dipper. The Milky Way spread its path of light above me and I sighed with great contentment.

After a while, soft, wispy clouds began to pass over the night sky. I returned to my cozy tent after a full day and fell asleep listening to nature's music. I sure love the Smokies.

Fun Facts About Fireflies
- Fireflies are not really flies, they are soft-bodied beetles.
- Not all members of the firefly family give off light as adults.
- All young (larvae) fireflies give off light.
- Even the eggs of some kinds of fireflies light up.

Activity Page

Venture's Favorite Constellations

Here are Venture's favorite star patterns.

Connect the stars to form the Little Bear. (It's also called the Little Dipper.) Go from 1 all the way to 8.

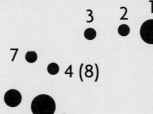

Now connect the stars to make the Big Dipper. (It's the brightest part of the Great Bear constellation.) Just go from A to H.

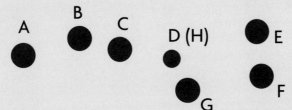

Notice how the two stars at the end of the Big Dipper point at the end of the Little Dipper. The bright star at the end of the Little Dipper's handle is called Polaris, and it shows the direction north. It's also called the North Star.

Activity Page

Design a Postcard

Design the front, back, and stamp of the postcard.
Write about the Smokies and address the card.

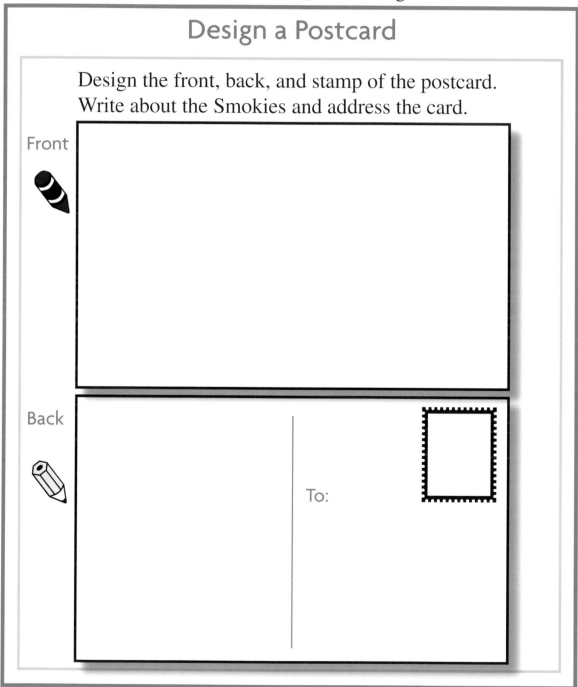

Front

Back

To:

Summer

Chapter 8

Lucky

Summer is a good time for adventure. Many of my adventures included a pony named Lucky. He is a great tour guide who likes exploring.

Lucky *looked* gentle and safe. I climbed into the saddle, took hold of the reins, and thought I would take a slow, calm ride.

Lucky thought otherwise! He was off and running in an instant. "Whoa!" I cried. *Bumpity, bumpity, bumpity, bump*, I bounced in the hard saddle. "Whoa, Lucky, whoa!"

I had to take control. I pulled hard on the reins. Lucky felt my tight grip and slowed down. Whew! I wanted to call him Not So Lucky. Had I chosen the wrong pony? But Lucky was his name and lucky he proved to be.

Lucky boldly clip-clopped along the sunlit trail. He seemed to know exactly what he wanted to show me.

On the first stop of his tour, I saw a magnificent male deer, or buck, browsing for flowers. His bony antlers were now covered with velvety hairs. In winter he would shed those antlers on the ground. Then squirrels and mice would happily gnaw on them to get calcium for their bodies. I admired his mighty antlers, but I was glad that I didn't have to wear such heavy things on my head.

As the buck searched for more to eat, he moved out of sight. Lucky and I continued on through the forest. I spied a strange-looking tree and inspected it closely. Deep claw marks scarred the trunk. Bear marks! Bears scratch trees and leave their scents to tell other bears to stay out of their space.

Lucky bravely continued to lead the way. We traveled along until he lowered his head and slowed to a stop. Lucky decided it was time for a long lunch and maybe a nap (if he could get away with it).

I slid down, tied him to a tree, and went searching for blackberries to eat. I found lots of juicy, ripe ones. I tossed each one in the air, eating them like popcorn. I hummed "Teddy Bears Picnic" as I moved from bush to bush with my wet, purple paws.

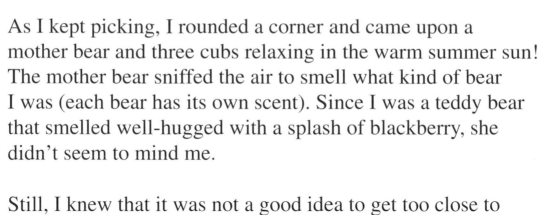

As I kept picking, I rounded a corner and came upon a mother bear and three cubs relaxing in the warm summer sun! The mother bear sniffed the air to smell what kind of bear I was (each bear has its own scent). Since I was a teddy bear that smelled well-hugged with a splash of blackberry, she didn't seem to mind me.

Still, I knew that it was not a good idea to get too close to a mother bear with her cubs, so I backed away. I returned to Lucky (who was well named after all) and thanked him for bringing me to this place of bears and berries.

I wanted to relax in the sun like the bears. I spread my blanket on the ground, stretched out on my back, and took a lovely, summer nap.

When I awoke, I opened my eyes to see yellow tiger swallowtails flying from flower to flower. They sipped sweet nectar with their long tongues. They enjoyed the warm sun too.

Lucky and I traveled back down the trail. To show my thanks to such a wonderful guide, I fed him apples, carrots, and lumps of sugar when we got home. Lucky and I have become great friends.

Fun Facts About Bears

- Boar is another name for a male bear.
- Sow is another name for a female bear.
- Adult bears weigh from 100 to 300 pounds. Male bears weigh more than females.
- Black bears can run up to 30 miles (48 kilometers) an hour.

Activity Page

Bears in the Smokies

What do you know about bears in the Smokies?
Draw or write your ideas in the boxes.

Bears in the
Smokies

Activity Page

Word Search
What Bears Eat

```
W E Z I A B R I V O U Y S I F E K T G M
B P Q G C B J G R A S S E S E S Q G L D L X
E S P J R L J T T I T M V J D P W I D M
L O A E C Q J H V N L A C O R N S K M K
E I N S E C T S C H E R R I E S H T L T
C B U Y E L L O W J A C K E T S B J X A
Y A R R L C R X Q F E X B J O H C D B N
C S Q T E B B A X D K N C I J Y S Z C T
H K M Q A H V T N Z R B M G Z U W X N S
E S Z U V E U F E H K G I J T A B O W M
S X A W E R O U L X M Z Z P Y A Z E C V
T R W G S Y O W L P M I N G O D D J K P
N P C R A N Z B S A L A M A N D E R S I
U C W U X Z B B E R R I E S R J G N A W
T D D B B M I C E H I C K O R Y N U T S
S K P S H G N J K R O O T S T W J A S G
Q W T A S N V P L X U R C J U T O C F Z
G X J L Y J N S Q U A W R O O T C M W J
H F C E W N Q Q F F N G A D Y K T Y T S
M F O Y K J X Q G R B U D S Q R F L U R
```

acorns	cherries	hickory nuts	grubs	roots	mice
insects	salamanders	buds	leaves	berries	
chestnuts	yellow jackets	grasses	ants	squawroot	

Autumn

Chapter 9
Autumn Adventures

The long days of summer came to an end and the year moved into autumn. It was the season of turning leaves. All around me, bright oranges, yellows, and reds dazzled my eyes. I opened them wide to take in all the beauty.

I knew this was the perfect time to visit the great elk in Cataloochee Valley. I wanted to see their large antlers and hear their loud mating calls.

Since Cataloochee is at the eastern edge of the park, I prepared for a full traveling day and got up before dawn. My backpack bulged with plenty of snacks for the long journey.

My first stop along the way was Roaring Fork Motor Nature Trail. I arrived as the sun began to rise. I found the sign to Grotto Falls and hiked through an old growth hemlock forest.

Mighty trees, hundreds of years old, towered above me. Unfortunately, aphid-like insects, called hemlock woolly adelgids, are killing these ancient trees. The insects, each smaller than the

head of a pin, drink the sap from the hemlock leaves. There are so many of them that the great trees weaken and die.

As I climbed higher along the path, I thought about the forest animals that need the hemlocks to shade the nearby streams. What will happen to these animals if the trees disappear? What will happen to the songbirds that use the high branches when passing through the Smokies in the spring and fall?

When I arrived at Grotto Falls, the powerful voice of the water soothed my troubled thoughts. I remembered that a lot of people who love the Smokies are trying to save the hemlock trees. I plan to be among them. I am, after all, a Junior Ranger. I pledged to protect the Smokies!

After gazing at the flowing waterfall for a long time, I followed the water back down the path. I found a place to have a snack on the shaded bank. As I rested, something brown moved into sight. I peered more closely and saw a sleek-coated mink search for its own snack in the water. A tasty crayfish would make its day.

The mink noticed me and hissed. Uh oh. Like a skunk, minks can spray an awful-smelling liquid when disturbed. I slowly got up and backed away while I still smelled huggable.

I left the land of the mink and mighty hemlock trees and continued on to see the elk. I had a long way to go, but I knew it would be worth the effort.

I arrived in the beautiful valley of Cataloochee and saw a huge herd of elk. I took out my binoculars and focused on a nearby bull (the male) and cow (the female). The antlers on that bull must have weighed more than 20 pounds.

As I watched, the bull threw back his head and let out a loud call. It started out like a low whistle and then built to a high-pitched squeal that seemed to fill the whole valley. Trying to attract the females, that bull put on quite a show.

The elk in this valley are very special. From 1750 until recently, no elk lived in this part of the Smokies. In 2001 and 2002, scientists brought many elk to Cataloochee to see if they would adapt to this new environment. It is still too early to tell if they will survive, but I sure hope they do.

After a full day, I arrived home and wrapped myself in warm clothes. I rocked on the porch, sipped hot cider, and wrote about my great autumn adventures in the Smokies.

Fun Facts About Elk

- Elk are members of the deer family.
- They eat grasses, acorns, bark, leaves, and buds.
- Male elk can have antlers up to five feet across.
- A male can weigh 700 to 1,100 pounds.

Activity Page

Words, Words, Words

?

How many words can your make from the letters in **Cataloochee Valley**?

?

Example: teach

_____   _____   _____   _____

_____   _____   _____   _____

_____   _____   _____   _____

_____   _____   _____   _____

_____   _____   _____   _____

_____   _____   _____   _____

_____   _____   _____   _____

_____   _____   _____   _____

_____   _____   _____   _____

_____   _____   _____   _____

_____   _____   _____   _____

_____   _____   _____   _____

Activity Page

Make a Map

Draw a map of the park.

Use the map in the front of the book as a guide.

➤ Write North at the top and South at the bottom.

➤ Write East on the right and West on the left.

➤ Write in Cataloochee and Roaring Fork Motor Nature Trail.

➤ Add your favorite places to visit.

Autumn

Chapter 10

Along the Creek to Abrams Falls

Thunder crashed and rain poured down one autumn morning. Luckily, I had rainwear for such a stormy day.

Waterproofed with my yellow raincoat, I headed off to Abrams Falls in Cades Cove. Since the Cherokee called Cades Cove *place of the river otter*, I wondered if I might see some of those playful animals there.

When I arrived at the trailhead by Abrams Creek, I read about Chief Abram. He was a Cherokee Indian chief who once

lived there. I could almost feel his presence in the woods. I imagined him gathering food, fishing in the creek, and hunting game. In his honor, I would walk softly on the land.

I treaded quietly and noticed many colorful mushrooms. I wondered whether Chief Abram would have eaten them, used them for medicine, or maybe made a dye from their colors. He would have called them by their Cherokee name, *da-wo-li*.

As I inspected the mushrooms, I heard distant drumming in the forest. What could it be? I followed the sound and the drumming grew louder and clearer.

I stopped, listened, and looked around. I noticed large holes in the trunks of the surrounding trees. Hmmm. What made those holes? I stayed still and didn't make a sound. I think Chief Abram would have been proud of my quiet listening skills.

Something flew from one high branch to another. I tracked it with my binoculars. I saw the large red-crested head of a bird almost the size of a crow. Its strong bill tapped on an old hollow tree. There was my drummer.

I took out my bird book, flipped through the pages, and found the bird I was looking at. It was a pileated woodpecker. I looked closer and saw bright red near its beak. That told me it was a male.

The woodpecker flew down and pecked at an old log on the ground. He picked up soggy leaves and flung them away as he tried to uncover insects. The woodpecker's long sticky tongue darted out and quickly captured a carpenter ant. Not what I would want for lunch, that's for sure.

After a while it flew off and I went to investigate the log. Ants hurried into holes for cover. I wondered about Chief Abram again. Did he hunt the pileated woodpecker for food? Did he use its feathers in a ceremony? I did know he called a woodpecker *da-la-la*.

Walking on, tiny prints in the muddy bank of the creek caught my attention. I followed them along the creek bank, careful not to make any noise. Finally, the tracks led into the water and I could not go any farther.

Suddenly, I heard splashing. I tracked the sound with my ears. Step by slow, cautious step, I crept over leaves and under limbs. As I rounded a bend, I met a river otter enjoying its watery world.

After splashing around, the otter got out and ran up the bank. Finding its smooth, muddy slide, it happily glided right back down and dove into the water. Otters love the water and are good swimmers. In fact, they can swim underwater for three or four minutes as they search for a meal of crayfish and slow-moving fish. Chief Abram called the otter *tsi-ya*.

The chief would have been happy to see the otters living and playing along his creek again. They disappeared in this area for many years after people killed them for their skins, logged the land, and clogged their streams with mud.

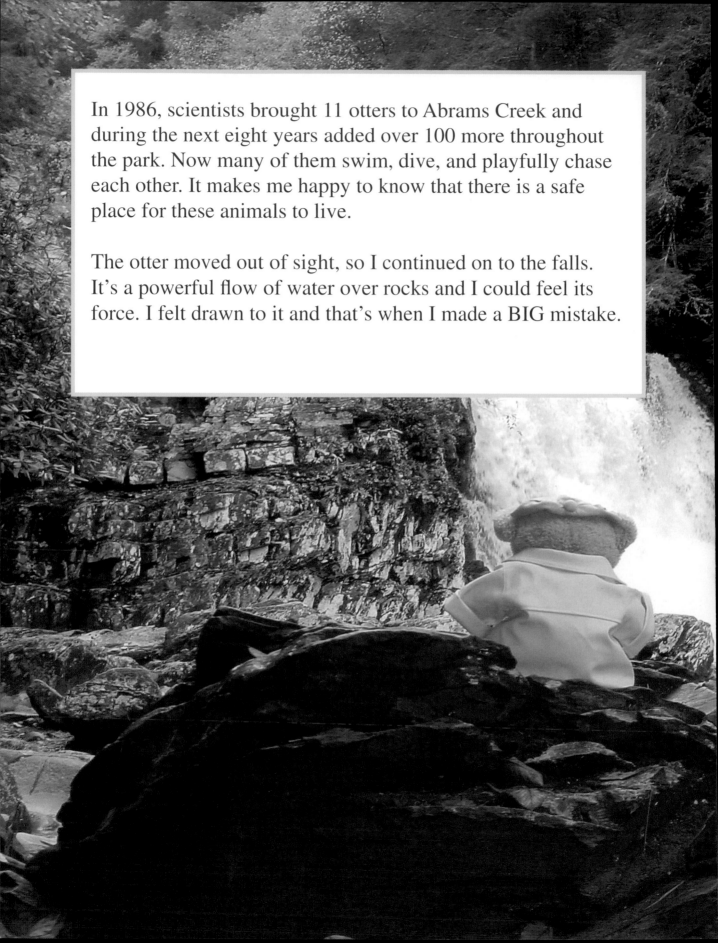

In 1986, scientists brought 11 otters to Abrams Creek and during the next eight years added over 100 more throughout the park. Now many of them swim, dive, and playfully chase each other. It makes me happy to know that there is a safe place for these animals to live.

The otter moved out of sight, so I continued on to the falls. It's a powerful flow of water over rocks and I could feel its force. I felt drawn to it and that's when I made a BIG mistake.

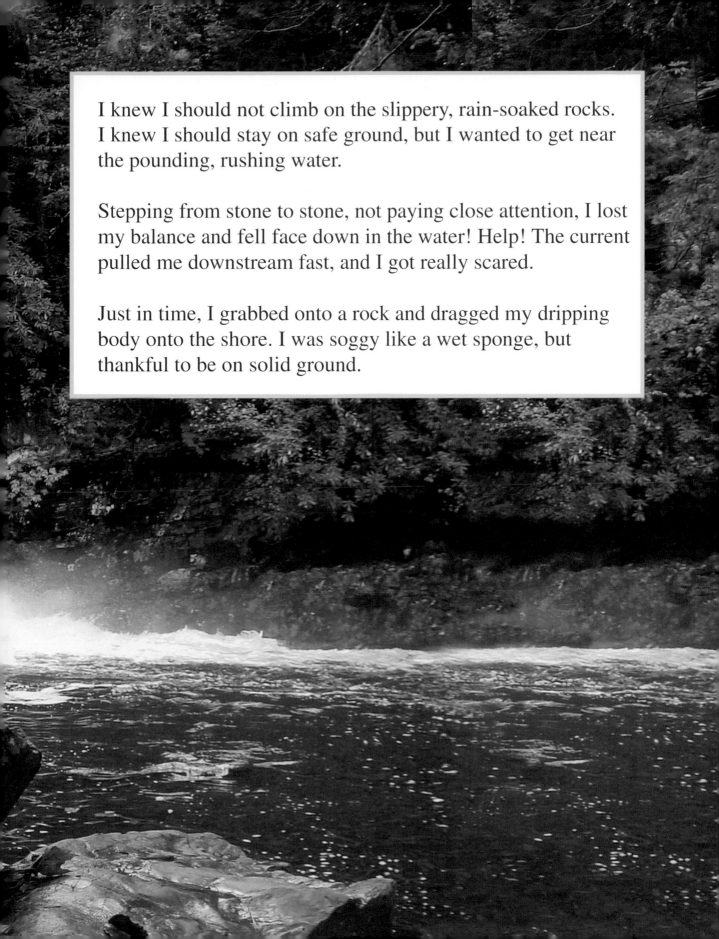

I knew I should not climb on the slippery, rain-soaked rocks. I knew I should stay on safe ground, but I wanted to get near the pounding, rushing water.

Stepping from stone to stone, not paying close attention, I lost my balance and fell face down in the water! Help! The current pulled me downstream fast, and I got really scared.

Just in time, I grabbed onto a rock and dragged my dripping body onto the shore. I was soggy like a wet sponge, but thankful to be on solid ground.

I vowed never to climb on slippery rocks again. Chief Abram would have been proud of me because I learned a very important lesson–**Safety First!**

I think the chief would call me *sensible bear.*

Fun Facts About Otters

- Otters are cousins to weasels, badgers, ferrets, minks, and skunks.
- They can weigh 10 to 25 pounds.
- An otter can be three to four feet long, including its tail.
- Pup is another name for a young otter.

Activity Page

My Favorite Animal

What is your favorite animal? _____

_____

What do you like about it? _____

_____

_____

_____

_____

_____

_____

_____

Draw your favorite animal.

Activity Page

Crossword
Abrams Creek

ACROSS

1. name for a young otter

3. an otter's cousin

5. food for an otter

7. crow-sized birds with red crest

DOWN

2. An otter can weigh 25
__ __ __ __ __ __.

4. Chief Abram spoke the
__ __ __ __ __ __ __ __
language.

6. another cousin of the otter

Autumn

Chapter 11
The Road to Newfound Wonders

Many visitors to the Smokies travel up and down Newfound Gap Road. There they find sunrises, sunsets, and mountain views. I like the word *newfound*. It reminds me to always look out for something new and exciting.

I packed my backpack carefully for a trip up the road. I remembered to bring my wool hat and scarf. The higher you go, the wetter, cooler, and windier it can get.

Up, up, up I went, marveling at the bright fall colors. As I climbed higher, spruce and fir trees came into view. I arrived at Newfound Gap, which is the highest point on the road at 5,046 feet.

There I looked over distant mountains that went on for miles. Newfound Gap marks the state line between North Carolina and Tennessee, so I saw mountains in two states.

President Franklin D. Roosevelt dedicated the Great Smoky Mountains National Park at Newfound Gap in 1940. At a big celebration he said, "We meet today to dedicate the mountains, streams, and forests to the service of the American people."

What a great day that was! The land and animals were protected. Hooray!

I heard there were even better views from Clingmans Dome, the highest point in the park at 6,643 feet above sea level. At the top you can see in every direction from a high tower. I found the trail and trudged up the steep, paved walkway. I stopped often to catch my breath.

It was a hard climb for a little bear like me. As I walked through ghostly fog, I saw many dead trees. Information signs along the way explained why the forest looked so sick. Balsam woolly adelgids (like those in the hemlocks) have killed almost all the Fraser fir trees. Also, air pollution in this area may have damaged the red spruce, fir, and other trees.

When I reached the high tower, I rested as I surveyed the mountains all around me. What a beautiful view. I thought about how President Roosevelt wanted to protect the Smokies. What would he have done to keep this forest healthy? I also wondered what I as a Junior Ranger could do to help the trees.

On my walk back down from the top, I took a side path and came upon the famous Appalachian Trail. It runs 2,144 miles from Maine to Georgia. Many strong hikers walk that whole trail from end to end. I would certainly save that long hike for another time!

As I thought about what it takes to make a long journey, a strong and mighty monarch butterfly flew over my head. Now there was an amazing traveler!

The incredible monarchs leave their summer homes in the north and fly south to Mexico in the fall. They fly all that way on four light wings flapping together. They weigh no more than a penny, yet are strong enough to fly great

distances. Many fly 2,000 miles one way!

How do these small, lightweight insects do it? Stored body fat gives them energy and strength for the long trip. Sometimes luck is with them and they hitch a ride on smooth-flowing winds. I wished that passing monarch good luck on its amazing journey.

After hiking some more, I paused for a hot chocolate break. No sooner had I relaxed when two bright eyes stared out at me from beneath a rotting log. The small, slimy body of a Jordan's (red-cheeked) salamander crawled out and made its way to a spot nearby. I had company.

Lucky for me the day was cool and misty. If the day had been hot, the salamander would not have come out. Salamanders breathe through their skin. Because of this, they need moisture and try to avoid sunshine and drying heat.

More than 30 kinds (species) of salamanders live in the forest and streams of the Smokies. Some people say this park is the salamander capital of the world. I wondered about my visitor. What would happen to it as the spruce-fir forest continued to change?

My new friend crawled away and disappeared under a rock, and I moved on. I looked forward to a much easier walk down the path. I felt honored to have seen this species of salamander. It lives in Great Smoky Mountains National Park and nowhere else on earth!

You don't want to miss Newfound Gap Road. You never know what wonderful new things you'll find there–or what new things will find you!

Fun Facts About Salamanders

- Salamanders are voiceless.
- They rely on smell to communicate with each other.
- Salamanders eat small insects, spiders, worms, and other things.

Activity Page

Nature's Wonders

What do you wonder about in nature? Write a sentence and draw a picture to describe what you're curious about.

I wonder _____

_____

_____

_____

_____

_____

_____

Draw what you're curious about.

Autumn

Chapter 12
Something Special

One beautiful fall day as I watched the leaves drift down, the phone rang. It was my friend Katie. I always like to hear from Katie. She is a scientist who studies bears. I learn a lot from her.

After we exchanged hellos, she said, "Venture, I have to test some of my equipment today. I thought you might like to see some of the ways I work with bears. I also want to show you something special. Do you have time for an adventure?"

I told her I would be ready in ten minutes. We arranged to meet at the Sugarlands trailhead. I gathered everything I might need and rushed to our destination.

When she arrived, she greeted me with a bright smile. "I can't wait to show you my surprise," she said, her eyes twinkling.

We climbed up the path, shuffling through crisp fallen leaves, until we stopped at a clear area. I watched with great interest as she spread some of her gear on the ground.

"Sometimes when I'm studying a bear," she said, "I first have to trap it. I don't hurt it. I just make it go to sleep for a little while. While it's dozing, I find out how old it is, how much it weighs, and whether it's healthy or sick. If it's a female, I place a collar around its neck. The collar falls apart in about three years."

She picked up a collar to show me. "The collar has a small, battery-powered radio transmitter that beeps. I can pick up the sound with this radio. I only collar females so I can find their dens in the winter. I see how many cubs they have. That helps me estimate the number of bears in the park."

She lifted an antenna and placed her radio close to my ear. "Listen," she said. I could hear a *beep, beep, beep* coming from a bear's collar far away. "I know that bear," she said. "Each bear collar has a different beep. This bear is about two miles from here. Maybe we'll run into her."

We tramped along and saw signs of bears everywhere, including scratch marks on fallen logs and tree trunks. "Sometimes bears scratch their fur against the bark," she told me. "Keep an eye out for bear fur."

"Also look for oak and hickory trees," Katie added. "This is the time when bears fatten up on acorns and nuts to prepare for their winter rest. Before they go into winter dens, they try to gain one to three pounds a day. This is the most important time for their survival."

Eating sounded like a good idea to me too. We relaxed by a small stream and nibbled trail mix.

As we rested, we gazed up into the canopy of the trees. I mentioned that the trees were very tall. Katie responded by saying, "I often need to climb to the tops of high trees like these to reach bear dens. I'll show you how I do it."

She got up and pulled some equipment from her bag. She threw a long rope up and around a high branch and clamped it on tightly. Then she struggled into a seat attached to the rope and lifted herself up with her strong, powerful arms.

"Now you try it," she said, offering me her gear. I managed to get into the seat and tried to balance myself. I pulled on the ropes, but nothing happened. "Here, let me help you," she said. She pulled on the rope and I found myself swinging high in the air. I didn't find any bear dens, but I could see that studying bears is hard work.

When I came down, Katie led me up a steep, leaf-covered hillside. I had a hard time keeping up. As we climbed higher, my legs wobbled and ached, and I began to pant.

I scrambled over fallen logs and tripped over jutting rocks. I crawled the last few feet to where Katie waited excitedly.

"Surprise!" she announced, pointing to an opening at the foot of an old hickory tree. "Welcome to a black bear den!"

A black bear den! Surprise was right! My tired body surged with excitement. Since most bear dens are high up in trees where a limb has broken off and rotted away, I felt very lucky to have one so close to the ground at the base of the tree.

Katie knew that no one was home (it was too early in the season for bears to be inside), so I ventured in myself. It was much larger than it looked from the outside. I felt the smooth, brown ground and touched the hard walls of the living tree. I was in a bear den!

"I found a mother and two small cubs in it a few years ago in February. The cubs only weighed about ten ounces," she reported. "They snuggled against their mother's fur and purred softly as they nursed. The mother didn't even move. It's amazing, but sometimes cubs are born while their mothers are still sleeping. She wakes up and there they are."

I rested inside in the cool darkness. It felt like home sweet home to me. I imagined sleeping most of the winter away in that sheltered place and wondered whether bears dream during that time, or even if they dream at all.

Katie interrupted my thoughts and said, "Well, it's about time we went home to our own dens, Venture. Was that steep climb worth it?"

I nodded my head and happily replied, "You bet!" I gave her a special bear hug and thanked her over and over again.

On the way back to the road I looked at other tree holes with new curiosity. What lived behind those little doorways? Was I passing other bear dens without knowing it?

As Katie and I parted, I felt glad that she had taught me so much and shown me something so special. But I think that Katie's hard work to help bears is the most special thing of all.

Fun Facts About Bear Births

- A mother bear usually has two cubs at a time.
- The cubs weigh one-half to one pound at birth.
- They are born blind and hairless.
- Their eyes open after about a month.

Activity Page

Figure it Out

??

A Cuddly Cub Problem

There were 126 female bears. Each gave birth to two cubs.

1. How many cubs were born? _____

2. How many bears (adults and cubs) were there altogether? _____

3. How did you figure it out?

_____

_____

_____

_____

_____

A Weighty Bear Problem

A female bear weighed 150 pounds. Then she ate lots of acorns and hickory nuts in the fall to prepare for the winter.

1. If she gained two pounds a day for 47 days, how much did she weigh altogether? _____

2. How did you figure it out?

_____

_____

_____

_____

_____

Activity Page

Bear Poster

Design a bear poster.

Winter

Chapter 13

Winter in the Smokies

As fall changed into winter, the days and nights grew colder. The trees lost their leaves, exposing the shapes of their sky-reaching branches.

I wandered through the woods and meadows, wearing my warm winter hat. The coldest season revealed its secrets in quiet ways. Time seemed to slow down. Even I slowed down, taking in nature's simple beauty. I began to hope for snow.

One day my wish came true. A thick blanket of clouds moved in during the night and the temperature dropped down very low. I awoke to cold winds and wet, white flakes. I stared up into the grey sky and watched the snowflakes drift softly down.

I wondered what all the animals were doing to keep warm and stay alive. I knew that some animals, like Canada geese, had left and traveled to warmer places. A few animals, like bats, were in a deep sleep called hibernation. Other animals, like rabbits, slept lightly, taking short winter naps when it got very cold outside.

After a few days the snow melted. I hiked in the woods and thought about the animals. Where were the fireflies and the songbirds? Where were the salamanders and the frogs?

I stopped to rest beside the clear waters of a stream. Lost in deep thought, the music of the water encouraged me to make up a little poem.

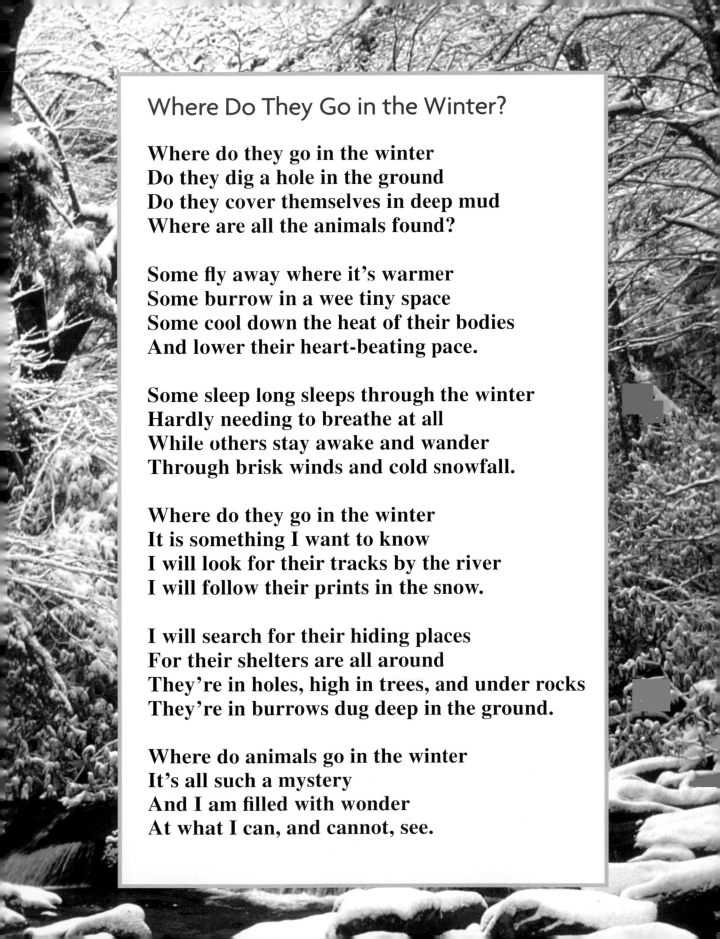

Where Do They Go in the Winter?

Where do they go in the winter
Do they dig a hole in the ground
Do they cover themselves in deep mud
Where are all the animals found?

Some fly away where it's warmer
Some burrow in a wee tiny space
Some cool down the heat of their bodies
And lower their heart-beating pace.

Some sleep long sleeps through the winter
Hardly needing to breathe at all
While others stay awake and wander
Through brisk winds and cold snowfall.

Where do they go in the winter
It is something I want to know
I will look for their tracks by the river
I will follow their prints in the snow.

I will search for their hiding places
For their shelters are all around
They're in holes, high in trees, and under rocks
They're in burrows dug deep in the ground.

Where do animals go in the winter
It's all such a mystery
And I am filled with wonder
At what I can, and cannot, see.

Like a song you can't get out of your mind, I repeated it over so many times that I knew I had to find some answers. I went searching for animal winter homes, humming "Where Do They Go in the Winter? " as I hiked along.

I spied a narrow deer trail and decided to follow its path. When I saw fresh deer tracks in some mud, I knew that the deer wasn't sleeping its winter away. It was eating bark, twigs, and the thin leaves of evergreen trees.

The deer trail led down to a stream. There I spied the work of beavers. It was obvious they weren't sleeping their winter away either. They used their sharp rodent teeth to cut trees to build a

dam. If the dam kept the stream from flowing, a pond would form. Many animals would enjoy the beaver-created wetland.

As I walked, I carefully stepped over a fresh raccoon print on the ground. That told me a raccoon was up and about. I also noticed some fox scat on a fallen log, so I knew that the fox wasn't sleeping either.

Then I came to a large entrance of a groundhog home. A groundhog is one of very few animals that hibernate all winter. It is a large stocky rodent with short legs and strong, digging claws. To dig its deep hole, it loosens the earth with its front claws and kicks the soil out of the tunnel with its back legs.

Somewhere in that dark, dark tunnel, the groundhog's house had many rooms, including a bedroom, side rooms, and even a toilet area. Was anyone home? Was there a groundhog down there, curled into a tight round ball, living off its body fat, deep asleep on warm grass and leaves?

Peering down into that dark hole, I knew that other animals might be down there too. Sometimes possums, skunks, weasels, rabbits, and even snakes use the groundhog's rooms to sleep or to hide from enemies.

Lucky for me I had discovered some animal signs and had learned a little more about what animals do in the winter. There was still so much to know and so much to explore.

As the winter days wore on, the air began to lose its chill. More and more sunlight warmed the earth. Soon spring would arrive with new flowers, singing birds, and bear cubs. I could hardly wait!

Fun Facts About Groundhogs

- Another name for the groundhog is woodchuck.
- When it hibernates, its heart rate slows down from its normal 80 beats per minute to about 5 beats per minute.
- During hibernation, its body temperature drops from its usual 100°F down to 30°F. It breathes only once every six minutes or so.
- Some groundhogs wake up during mild weather.

Activity Page

Where Do They Go?

Choose a favorite verse from Venture's winter poem and illustrate it.

_____

_____

_____

_____

_____

_____

_____

Activity Page

Write Your Own Verse

Make up your own verse to Venture's winter poem and illustrate it.

_____

_____

_____

_____

_____

_____

_____

Chapter 14
Look for Me in the Smokies

Look for me in the Smokies
A brown little teddy bear
Always ready for adventure
You know that I'll be there.

You might find me in the woodlands
Or meadows where deer like to roam
You might see me by the river
In search of a beaver home.

You might spy me with my journal
Taking notes on what I see
Or catch me with hot chocolate
Reciting poetry.

Maybe you'll find me grinding corn

And baking my own bread

Or sitting on an old farm porch

After the cows are fed.

I'll be there in the springtime

When the cubs come out to play

I'll be fishing in cool waters

On a sizzling summer day.

In the fall I'll climb up mountains

That are high and very steep

In winter I'll be wanting

To know where the animals sleep.

So look for me in the Smokies

With a pack upon my back

Bulging with all things useful

Especially an afternoon snack.

I'll be there in the Smokies

It's where I want to be

With wonders all around

It's the perfect place for me.

It's the perfect place for you, as well

I hope to see you there

So keep your eyes wide open

For a small brown teddy bear.

Venture,

the traveling teddy bear,

wishing you beauty

in your life,

everyday and

everywhere.

Groups to Contact for More Information

Great Smoky Mountains Association
115 Park Headquarters Road
Gatlinburg, TN 37738
www.SmokiesStore.org
1-865-436-7318

Friends of GSMNP
PO Box 5650
Sevierville, TN 37864
www.friendsofthesmokies.org
1-865-453-2428

Great Smoky Mountains Institute at Tremont
Great Smoky Mountains National Park
9275 Tremont Road
Townsend, TN 37882
www.gsmit.org
1-865-448-6709

To Order Venture to the Smokies
and your own Venture the traveling teddy bear™

web: www.venturesadventures.com

email: info@venturesadventures.com

phone: 541-543-7498

fax: 541-343-0194

address: Venture's Adventures, LLC
2406 Lawrence Street
Eugene, OR 97405-2660

Activity Answers

Page 5:

Word Scramble

1. PAMS — m a p s
2. SEPNLCI — p e n c i l s
3. OTH LAETOCOHC — h o t   c h o c o l a t e
4. LNRJUOA — j o u r n a l
5. CBKAKACP — b a c k p a c k
6. RUISAOLBCN — b i n o c u l a r s
7. NETT — t e n t
8. ITALFLHHSG — f l a s h l i g h t
9. AHT — h a t
10. RCAEAM — c a m e r a

Page 11:

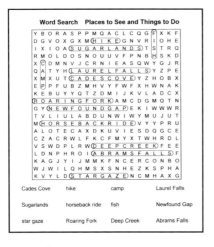

Word Search   Places to See and Things to Do

Cades Cove — hike — camp — Laurel Falls
Sugarlands — horseback ride — fish — Newfound Gap
star gaze — Roaring Fork — Deep Creek — Abrams Falls

Page 12:

Page 22:

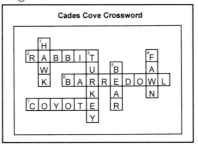

Cades Cove Crossword

Page 36:

Work and Play on the Farm Scramble

1. YLPA — p l a y
2. IDRE — r i d e
3. DEACN — d a n c e
4. FEDE — f e e d
5. KBAE — b a k e
6. BDLIU — b u i l d
7. IMLK — m i l k
8. NPA — n a p
9. CILBM — c l i m b
10. HOPC — c h o p
11. POWL — p l o w
12. AGZE — g a z e

Page 44:

What Green Frogs Eat Word Search

Activity Answers

Page 60:

Word Search   Some Things Bears Eat

Page 67:

a	coal	hello	locate
ache	coat	ho	loot
ahoy	cool	hoe	lot
ale	coot	hole	love
all	cove	holly	lovely
alley	covey	holy	oat
aloe	coy	hoot	oval
at	each	hove	tale
atoll	eat	hot	tall
call	eaves	hove	tally
cat	eel	lace	tea
catch	elect	lacy	teach
cave	eve	latch	teal
cay	hale	late	the
cell	hall	late	they
chat	halt	lathe	tool
cheat	halve	lava	toy
cheetah	hat	lay	vale
choo	hatch	leach	vat
clay	hate	leach	veal
clay	have	leave	vet
cleat	hay	leave	vetch
cleave	hay	lee	vole
clot	he	leech	vote
cloth	heal	let	yeah
clothe	heat	levee	yell
clove	heave	level	yet
cloy	heavy	levy	
coach	heel	local	

Page 78:

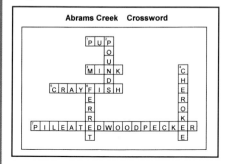

Abrams Creek   Crossword

Page 95:

A Cuddly Cub Problem:
There were 126 female bears.
Each gave birth to two cubs.
1. How many cubs were born? 252
2. How many bears (adults and cubs) were there altogether? 378

A Weighty Bear Problem:
A female bear weighed 150 pounds.
Then she ate lots of acorns and hickory nuts in the fall to prepare for the winter.
1. If she gained two pounds a day for 47 days, how much did she weigh altogether? 244